START-UP
DESIGN AND TECHNOLOGY

PLAYGROUND EQUIPMENT

Louise and Richard Spilsbury

Evans

Published by Evans Brothers Limited
2A Portman Mansions
Chiltern Street
London W1U 6NR

© Evans Brothers Limited 2006

Produced for Evans Brothers Limited by
White-Thomson Publishing Ltd.,
Bridgewater Business Centre, 210 High Street,
Lewes, East Sussex BN7 2NH

Printed in China by WKT Company Limited

Editor: Dereen Taylor
Consultants: Nina Siddall, Head of Primary School
Improvement, East Sussex; Norah Granger, former
primary head teacher and senior lecturer in Education,
University of Brighton
Designer: Leishman Design

British Library Cataloguing in Publication Data
Spilsbury, Louise
  Playground equipment. - (Start-up design &
technology)
  1.Playgrounds - Equipment and supplies -
  Juvenile literature
  I.Title
  769'.068

ISBN-10: 0 237 53023 6
13-digit ISBN (from 1 Jan 2007) 978 0 237 53023 5

Acknowledgements:
Special thanks to the following for their help and
involvement in the preparation of this book: Staff
and pupils at Coldean Primary School, Brighton;
Elm Grove Primary School, Brighton; Hassocks
Infants School, Hassocks.

Picture Acknowledgements:
Liz Price 5 (left), 7 (bottom), 10, 11,
14 (left), 15; Alamy 18.
All other photographs by Chris Fairclough.

Artwork:
Hattie Spilsbury, age 10, pages 6 and 19.

Special thanks to:
Tessa Coulthard of Stokenham Area Primary School.

Contents

At the playground 4

Playground shapes 6

Making a see-saw 8

Moving in a playground 10

Making a roundabout 12

Playground materials 14

A playground pictogram 16

Planning a model swing 18

Making a model swing 20

Further information for Parents and Teachers 22

Index 24

At the playground

Do you know the names of the playground equipment in this playground? Who would enjoy playing in this playground?

Why do we have playgrounds?

playground   equipment

What equipment do you like playing on best?

"I like the rocker best. It moves really fast!"

"I like the bars because I can swing on them!"

rocker   bars

Playground shapes

Pradip has drawn a picture of a climbing frame. He adds labels that name the shape of the different parts. How many of each shape can you see in the picture?

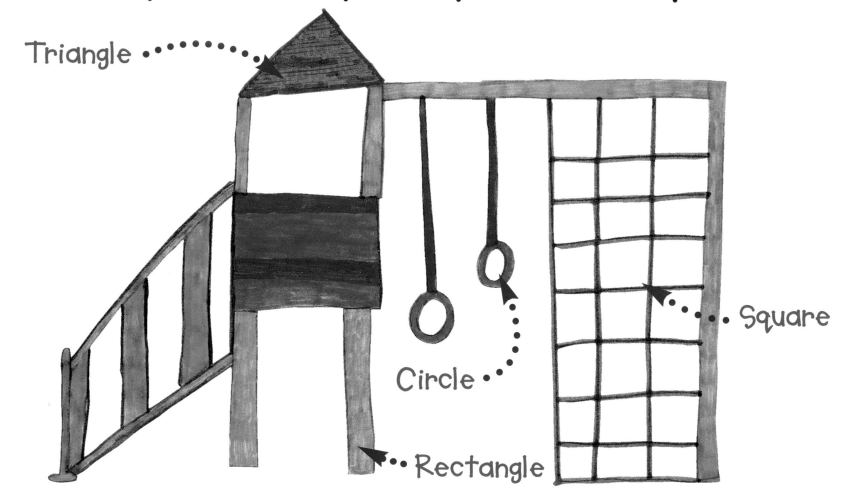

Triangle

Circle

Rectangle

Square

Which playground equipment would you draw?

6 circle triangle square rectangle

A **framework** helps **structures** stand up. Frameworks can be different shapes.

▶ **This train has round wooden wheels that help it stand up. The wheels make the train stable and able to support a load.**

◀ **The legs of this table make a triangle framework. Can you find anything in your house or garden with a square framework?**

Making a see-saw

Jo's class have been singing 'See-saw, Margery Daw'. Jo is planning how to make a model see-saw.

▶ She tests paper and card for the seat. She chooses to use card because the paper is too bendy.

Materials and tools
- card • paper
- scissors • Plasticine
- silver foil

◀ She carefully cuts out the card seat.

▶ She uses a card triangle for the base. She uses Plasticine to stick the seat to the base.

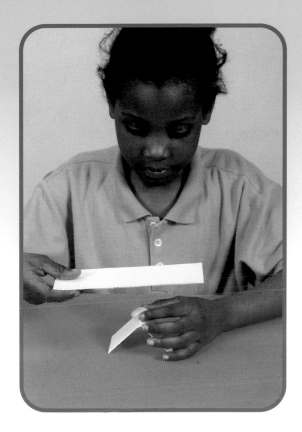

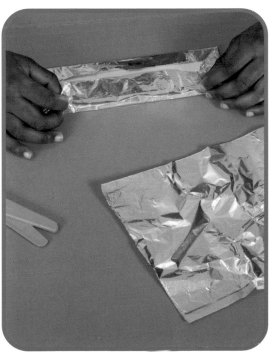

◀ Jo decorates it with foil so that it looks more like a real see-saw.

▶ She tests her model to see how it moves.

scissors   base   decorates   moves   9

Moving in a playground

You push a roundabout to start it moving. It turns round and round. When you push harder, the roundabout goes faster.

▲ Kira pulls on the bars to slow down the roundabout and stop it. Pushes and pulls are forces.

push   turns   faster   pulls   slow

▼ **Tom pushes Will on the swing. The swing goes** backwards **and** forwards.

▼ **You don't need pushes and pulls on a slide. Dan slides down. To slow down or stop he holds on to the sides.**

stop forces backwards forwards **11**

Making a roundabout

Ali wants to make a model roundabout.

▲ He has drawn round a plate on card. He cuts out the circle.

▲ He puts Plasticine in the middle of the card. Then he pushes the tip of a pencil through the card into the Plasticine to make a hole.

split pin   cotton reel

▲ Ali **improves** his roundabout by sticking on **pipe cleaners** to make bars. When Ali pushes the bars, the roundabout turns round.

▲ Ali removes the Plasticine and puts a **split pin** through the hole and into a **cotton reel**.

Could Ali make the roundabout look more fun to use?

improves   **pipe cleaners**   13

Playground materials

The labels on this swing and rocker show some of the different materials playground equipment is made from.

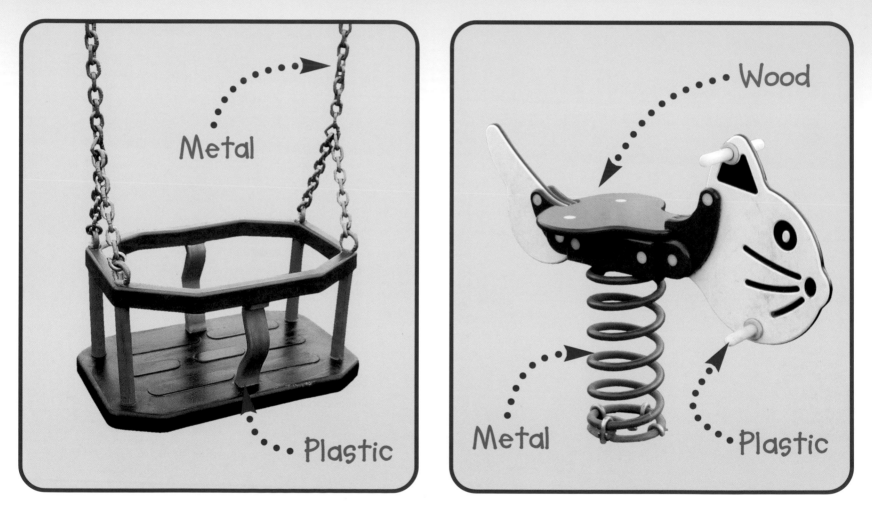

Metal

Plastic

Wood

Metal

Plastic

There are three different materials. What are they?
Why were they chosen?

materials   describe   smooth

There are lots of different words to describe how materials look or feel.
Which words would you choose to describe these playground materials?

bendy   smooth   shiny   stiff   rough

cold   waterproof   hard   worn

shiny   rough   cold   waterproof

A playground pictogram

▶ **Fatima asked children in her class about their favourite playground equipment.**

◀ **She entered the information onto the computer. She used the mouse to select playground icons. She sorted the information into a pictogram.**

information   mouse   select

The number of ticks in each column shows how many children chose each piece of playground equipment. Which is the most popular piece of equipment? How many more people chose the swing than the slide?

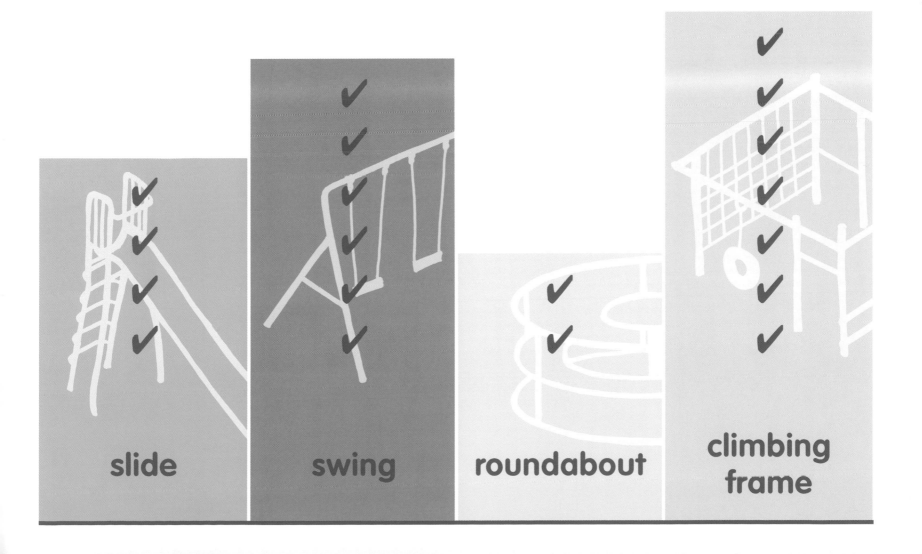

slide   swing   roundabout   climbing frame

icons   sorted   pictogram

Planning a model swing

Max is looking at pictures to get ideas for a model swing.

Max wants to design a swing for his little sister. Which one do you think he chooses?

ideas   design   sketch   weight

Max plans his model carefully. He draws a sketch of his design. He makes a list of all the materials he will need.

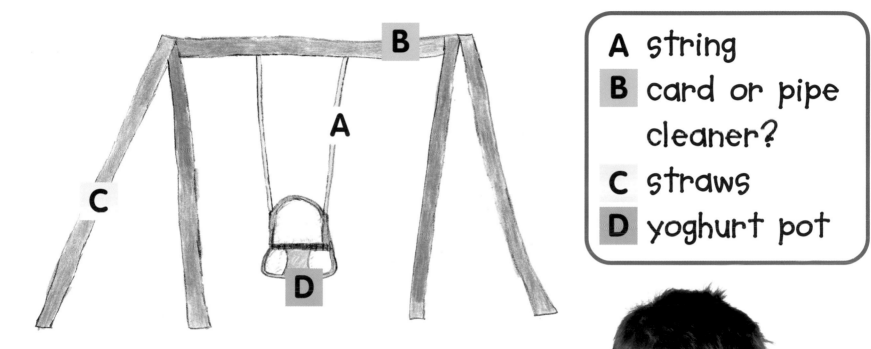

A string
B card or pipe cleaner?
C straws
D yoghurt pot

Max wants the swing framework to be strong and stable. He tests a pipe cleaner and a piece of card to see which can take more weight.

Making a model swing

First Max makes the framework for the swing.

◀ **Max uses a plier punch to make a hole in each corner of the card and two in the middle. Next he makes two holes in the yoghurt pot.**

▶ **He pushes straws through the four corner holes.**

plier punch

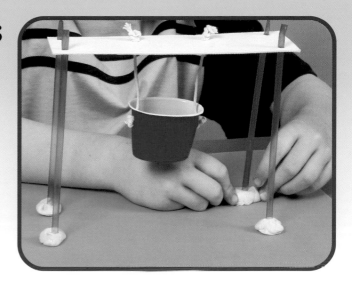

▶ **Max ties the pot to the card. He improves his model by putting Plasticine under the legs to make it more stable.**

▲ **He threads string through the holes in the pot and ties a knot at one end.**

▶ **Does Max's model look like his sketch on page 19? Why do you think this is?**

knot   stable   **21**

Further information for

New words listed in the text:

backwards	design	information	planning	select	stop
bars	equipment	knot	playground	shiny	structures
base	faster	load	plier punch	sketch	tests
bendy	forces	materials	pulls	slow	triangle
circle	forwards	model	push	smooth	turns
cold	framework	mouse	rectangle	sorted	waterproof
cotton reel	icons	moves	rocker	split pin	weight
decorates	ideas	pictogram	rough	square	
describe	improves	pipe cleaners	scissors	stable	

Possible Activities

PAGES 4-5

Children could visit a shop to look at smaller items of playground equipment that are sold for gardens or homes and talk about how these differ from municipal playground equipment.

Look at pictures of different sorts of playgrounds, such as those for very young children, or older children or those based on a particular theme, such as pirates. Discuss who the playgrounds are designed for, and how they know this.

PAGES 6-7

Show children how to make a square or rectangular frame using construction kits. You could talk about how to make frames more stable and able to carry greater loads by adding extra parts or by adding supports. Get the children to assess their own frame and each other's.

Ask the children to cut out or download pictures of parts of playground equipment and group them according to their shape.

PAGES 8-9

Children could try making their own see-saw using different shapes for the base, such as a cylinder, and using construction kits.

Ask children to think of other nursery rhymes or songs that they could sing in the playground, such as 'Rock-a-bye-Baby' or 'Swing low, sweet chariot'.

PAGES 10-11

Visit a local playground and talk about the different ways in which pieces of playground equipment move or the way we move when we play on them. They could think of other words to describe the different movements. Also talk about the other things that cause movement. For example, look at the way wind blows leaves around the playground.

PAGES 12-13

Ask the children to construct a slide using bricks from a construction kit. Show the children that a strip of card could be used for the slide part to make it more slippery. Try out the slide using a model figure.

Parents and Teachers

PAGES 14-15

Ask the children to group parts of playground equipment according to the different materials from which they are made. They could sort the materials into a chart and make a third column saying what properties the materials have, eg waterproof, strong.

Children could collect and test some different materials to see which is waterproof, hard-wearing, etc, and therefore suitable for outdoor play equipment.

PAGES 16-17

Using the computer, children could design a poster advertising a new playground or park using words and possibly pictures that persuade children to use it. Children could select words from a computer word bank to type a few sentences about playgrounds.

PAGES 18-19

Children could design and draw on paper or on the computer a fantasy playground with a particular theme or person in mind. Or they could use clipart/stamps/motifs to design a playground, using the mouse to move and place items accurately on screen.

PAGES 20-21

Get the children to make their own pieces of individual playground equipment that can be put together on a table to make a playground display. This also gives the children a chance to think about playground surfaces, which are often covered in materials such as wood chips, leading to a discussion about safety in the playground.

Further Information

BOOKS FOR CHILDREN

Forces and Movement (Start-up Science)
Claire Llewellyn, Evans, 2004

How Do They Work? Playground Equipment
Wendy Sadler, Heinemann Library, 2006

Materials (Start-up Science)
Claire Llewellyn, Evans, 2004

Playground Science: Pack of 6 (Four Corners)
Elizabeth Paren, Longman, 2004

Pushing (Read and Learn: Investigations)
Patricia Whitehouse, Raintree, 2004

Sliding (Investigations)
Patricia Whitehouse, Raintree, 2004

WEBSITES

www.planetscience.com

Index

b

bars 5

c

climbing frame 6, 17
computer 16
cutting 9, 12

d

designing 18, 19
drawing 6, 12, 19

f

forces 10, 11
frameworks 7, 19, 20

m

materials 8, 9, 12, 13, 14, 15, 19

models 8, 9, 12, 13, 18, 19, 20, 21
movement 10, 11

p

pictogram 16, 17
planning 8, 18, 19
Plasticine 9, 12, 13, 21
play equipment 4, 5, 6, 14, 15, 16, 17
playgrounds 4, 5, 10, 11

r

rocker 5, 14
roundabouts 10, 12, 13, 17

s

scissors 8, 9, 12
see-saw 8, 9
shapes 6, 7

sketches 19, 21
slides 11, 17
sorting 16
sticking 9, 13
swings 11, 14, 17, 18, 19, 20, 21

t

testing 8, 9, 19
tools 8, 13